THINKABOUT
Seeing

Text: Henry Pluckrose
Photography: Chris Fairclough

Franklin Watts

London/New York/Sydney/Toronto

© 1986 Franklin Watts Limited

First published in the USA by
Franklin Watts Inc.
387 Park Avenue South
New York, N.Y. 10016
US ISBN: 0-531 101711

Editor: Ruth Thomson
Design: Edward Kinsey
Additional Photographs: Zefa
Sally Anne Thompson
Hatfield Polytechnic Observatory
All Action Photographic

Typesetting: Keyspools

Printed in Belgium

About this book

Parents can share the book with young children. Its aim is to bring into focus some of the elements of life and living which are all too often taken for granted. To develop fully, all young children need to have their understanding of the world deepened and the language they use to express their ideas extended. This book takes the everyday things of the child's world and explores them, harnessing curiosity and wonder in a purposeful way.

For those working with young children each book is designed to be used both as a picture book, which explores ideas and concepts, and as a starting point to talk and exploration. The pictures have been selected because they are of interest in themselves and also because they include elements which will promote enquiry. Talk can lead to displays of items and pictures collected by children and teacher. Pictures and collages can be made by the children themselves.

Everything in our environment is of interest to the growing child. The purpose of these books is to extend and develop that interest.

Henry Pluckrose.

Shut your eyes tightly.
Keep them closed for a moment.
What can you see?
Without sight, you would be blind.
You would not be able to see.

Our eyes are like windows.
They let us look out
on the world.

Our eyes can see tiny things like the pattern on the back of a ladybug

and enormous things
like this elephant.

Our eyes can see things
far away
and things near at hand.

Far away,
even large things
look small.

Our eyes help us to understand
the things around us –
to tell us whether things are hard
or soft,

and whether things are easy
or difficult to reach.

Here the moon looks like
a tiny ball in the sky.

But through a telescope
it looks like this.

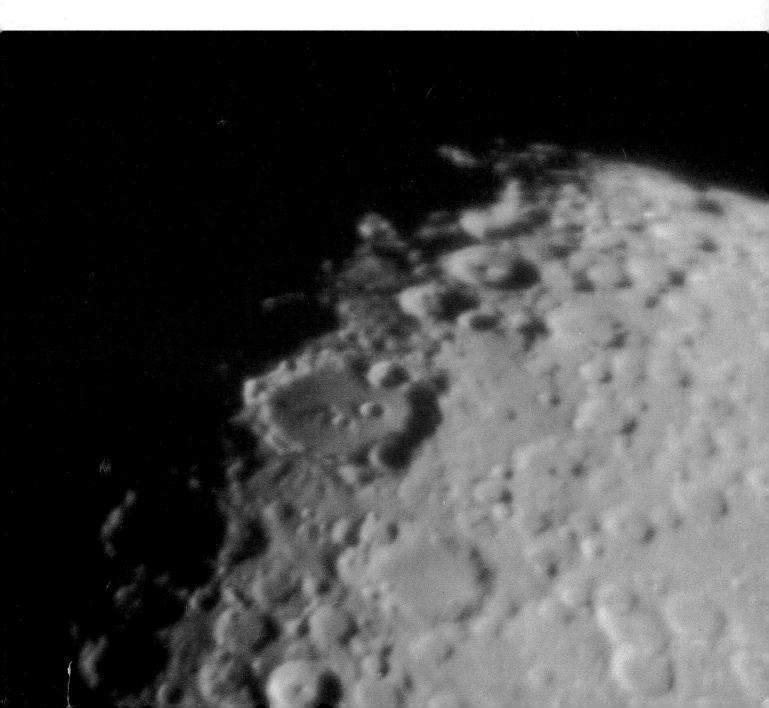

The world is full of color.
Our eyes recognize color.
Which colors do you like most?

Which colors
do you like to use
in your paintings?

Some colors are used
to give messages.
Red often means "Stop!"

Green often means "Go."

We never stop using our eyes
except when we are asleep.
We use them when playing
with friends,

when riding a bike,

when watching a show,

when looking at books.

Without sight,
people could not drive
cars or buses

or use great machines.

Not everybody has perfect sight.
Some people need to wear glasses.
Glasses help the eyes to see
more clearly.

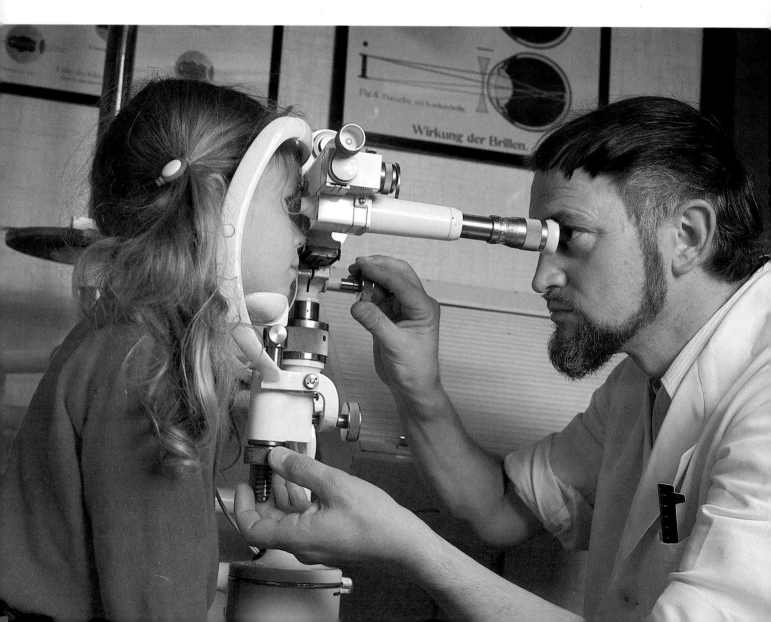

Sometimes people become blind.
Dogs can be trained to lead them.

To see, our eyes need light.
During daytime,
the light comes from the sun.

When darkness falls,
we need artificial light
to help us to see.

Shut your eyes tightly.
Keep them closed for a moment.
What can you see?
Open your eyes.
Look and see.